THE ULTIMATE CLUBHOUSE PLAYBOOK

Make Powerful Connections to Secure Your Next Promotion or Get More Clients and Customers

Adriane Simpson

The Ultimate Clubhouse Playbook: Make Powerful Connections to Secure Your Next Promotion or Get More Clients and Customers

Copyright © 2021 The LinkedIn Pros

All Rights Reserved. Published 2021.

Edited by Author Coach and Book Editor Candice L. Davis, CandiceLDavis.com

No part of this publication may be reproduced, distributed, or transmitted in any form or by any means, including photocopying, recording, or other electronic or mechanical methods, without the prior written permission of the publisher, except in the case of brief quotations embodied in critical reviews and certain other noncommercial uses permitted by copyright law. For permission requests, write to the publisher, addressed "Attention: Permissions Coordinator," at support@thelinkedinpros.com.

This book is presented solely for educational and entertainment purposes. The author and publisher are not offering it as financial, marketing, or other professional services advice. While best efforts have been used in preparing this book, the author and publisher make no representations or warranties of any kind and assume no liabilities of any kind with respect to the accuracy or completeness of the contents and specifically disclaim any implied warranties of merchantability or fitness of use for a particular purpose. Neither the author nor the publisher shall be held liable or responsible to any person or entity with respect to any loss or incidental or consequential damages caused, or alleged to have been caused, directly or indirectly, by the information or programs contained herein. Every individual is different, and the advice and strategies contained herein may not be suitable for your situation. The story and its characters are an amalgam of the author's own experiences. Other results may vary.

First published by LinkedIn Pros, The

ISBN: 978-1-7368433-0-7

Printed in the United States of America

The LinkedIn Pros
www.thelinkedinpros.com

CONTENTS

This Book Is for People Who Want More out of Work
and Business 1

Working the System............................3

1 **Clubhouse, It's More Than a Hangout Spot** ... 11
   What Is Clubhouse, Really?.....................13
   Why You Should Be on Clubhouse ASAP.........16
   Potential Pitfalls and How to Avoid Them 17

2 **Get Comfortable on Clubhouse** 19
   How to Get on Clubhouse 21
   Your Clubhouse Profile 24
   Who to Follow................................ 27
   Invites 29
   Welcoming New Users......................... 31
   Rooms....................................... 31
   The Stage.................................... 34

3	**But First, a Necessary Detour to LinkedIn**	**37**
	Get on LinkedIn	41
	Your LinkedIn Profile	41
	Making Connections	54
	The Numbers Matter	59
	Inviting Strangers to Connect	61
	Accepting Connections	62
	Posting on LinkedIn	64
	How to Make the Most of LinkedIn	65
4	**Create Your Clubhouse Strategy**	**67**
	Set Specific Clubhouse Goals	69
	Your Strategy	71
5	**Share Your Expertise & Stand Out**	**73**
	Speak Up	74
	Start a Room	78
	Start a Club	85
	Join a Club	88
	Finding Places to Be	89
6	**The Secret to Maximizing Clubhouse**	**91**
	Validate and Leverage Clubhouse with LinkedIn	92
	The Elephant in the Room	97
	The Future of Clubhouse and LinkedIn	99
Resources		**103**

THIS BOOK IS FOR PEOPLE WHO WANT MORE OUT OF WORK AND BUSINESS

Most of the business books you'll find on real and virtual bookshelves are written either for employees climbing the corporate ladder *or* for entrepreneurs who want to start or grow a business.

This book is for both corporate professionals and business owners. If you want more from your work—whether you work for yourself or someone else—this book is for you.

Whatever your professional goals are, used wisely, social media can help you accomplish them. Clubhouse in particular offers entrepreneurs, executives, and professionals unlimited avenues to get clients and customers, secure a dream job, or find new ways to increase income.

This book is for people who want to leverage this unique new platform, have fun doing it, and still have time left to do your job or run your business.

This book is for people who want more—and want to take full advantage of Clubhouse to get it faster.

Visit bit.ly/ClubhouseQuickStart to download my free resource for readers. These checklists, trackers, and process maps will help you implement everything you read here without missing a step.

WORKING THE SYSTEM

I was working remotely, and I'll confess, not giving my full attention to the Zoom call. In fact, I was only half listening while I got some work done, so I almost missed the announcement. Had I really heard that everyone on that call, including me, was getting laid off? Once that fact registered in my brain, I quickly switched gears from finishing my work to updating my resume. Unlike many people, I didn't feel a sense of panic. I'd been laid off before—a total of four times during the course of my career—and I knew I'd be fine. Things would work out for me, I knew, because I had a system.

Things did work out for me, so much so that I started teaching other people how to do exactly what I'd done several times over. I launched my business, The LinkedIn Pros, and started coaching professionals to find their dream jobs, maximize every job offer, and increase their income by five or even six figures with one job move. It didn't matter what field they were in. My clients work in technology, pharmaceuticals, health care, the beauty industry, education, politics, government, and the nonprofit sector. And my system works for all of them—as long as they work the system.

Not long after I started coaching corporate clients, I said yes to consulting with small business owners who needed help growing their business. These clients are public speakers and professional coaches. They work in retail, have medical practices, and run beauty brands. While their goals are different, most of the same principles apply. I customize my system to suit their needs, and the system works for these entrepreneurs too.

It has been a long while since I was in the market for a job, but every day, I get DMs in my inbox from people who want to recruit me for a position in their company. The opportunities are abundant even when the economy seems shaky. I used to forward all those messages to my friends and colleagues, but these days, I can't keep up with them. I forward what I can, but much to my disappointment, I have to leave many of them unanswered.

I've spent most of my career connecting people across my network to help them achieve their professional goals. It's instinctive for me to share job opportunities with people who may be interested in them or introduce two people who can benefit from meeting. My bent for making productive introductions is how I wound up with the nickname "Queen of the Warm Handshake." I recognized, early on, the value of relationships in accelerating your career growth or growing your business, and I've been shaking hands and passing names ever since. That, as you'll see, is why I love Clubhouse.

Every time a new social media app pops up, internet gurus promise it can help us earn more money somehow. Corporate ladder-climbers flock to the platform looking to expand their professional network and land a better job. Entrepreneurs get onboard to try to find more clients or sell more of their products. Inevitably, some small percentage of users get great results, but most people don't get far. They meet new people, but those relationships don't go anywhere. They attract lots of followers, but they struggle to monetize that following. Or they create a system that works only to have the platform change the rules and wipe out their system completely. (Business owners, remember when

Facebook used to show all your page posts to your followers for free?)

The good news is that Clubhouse is different. This social media platform was developed to give people a place to be heard, to discuss topics that matter to them, to create new connections, and to have meaningful conversations. That last goal is a game changer. The app is still in its early days, of course, but Clubhouse is a powerful tool, and as you'll see as you read on, its effectiveness is magnified exponentially when you combine it with the power of LinkedIn. (If you're not a LinkedIn fan because you find it boring or stuffy, you're not the only one. But stick with me. I'll show you why it works and how to work it.)

In just a few months since joining Clubhouse, I've gained hundreds of LinkedIn connections simply by sharing my LinkedIn profile link in my Clubhouse bio and inviting people in rooms to find me on LinkedIn. I've also added dozens of Instagram followers and connected with more than fifty people offline. Some of those connections have led to speaking opportunities, successful pitches, and the start of ongoing relationships with potential clients and strategic partners. And I've accomplished all this without any direct selling on the platform.

Clubhouse has allowed me to engage in conversation with my audience in ways I can't on other platforms. While I went all in and spent several hours a day on the platform when I first joined, I quickly scaled back my time there. Even as I spend less time on Clubhouse, I've created a solid reputation on the platform so that when I go into rooms, I'm likely to be called on stage to share my expertise. While I can't always say yes to the opportunity, I always appreciate it.

The good news is that you don't have to invest the amount of time I did to get similar or even better results. I wrote this book to give you a leg up on leveraging Clubhouse to achieve your professional goals by using the same strategies that have worked for my clients, my colleagues, and me.

If you're a corporate professional, the strategies in this book can help you:

1. Find your dream job in your current industry or a whole new field.
2. Increase your salary by making the leap to a new company.
3. Solidify your reputation as the expert in your role.

4. Expand your professional network for future sales and partnerships.
5. Demonstrate your value to your current employer and position yourself for raises and promotions.

If you're an entrepreneur, these strategies can help you:

1. Attract new clients without spending money on ads.
2. Sell more of your products to your target market.
3. Position yourself as the expert in your current niche or a new niche.
4. Grow your list of email subscribers.
5. Find strategic partners and establish new affiliate relationships or joint-venture partnerships.

I've used these strategies to land new jobs that increased my income by multiple five figures and to accelerate the growth of my business. I've also walked my coaching clients through these steps to accomplish their own goals as corporate professionals and entrepreneurs. The technology behind Clubhouse will inevitably change. In fact, some of the user interface may have changed by the time you read this. However, what I'll share with you isn't dependent on the interface. These strategies have worked for me and my clients for years now, and they'll continue to work far into the future. Clubhouse has just given us new ways to maximize them.

Social media has become an integral part of my relationship building over the last several years. But I don't use it frivolously. The true value of social media is always in building relationships of various kinds. To make the most of Clubhouse, you should be social—connecting and engaging—but you also need to be strategic and intentional. You need a plan. This book will help you customize a plan to achieve your goals. It's never too early or too late to get started, but starting sooner means getting results more quickly. Get started now.

chapter 1
CLUBHOUSE, IT'S MORE THAN A HANGOUT SPOT

When Joy Pittman (@oliviapopeofhr), founder of HR for the Culture, joined Clubhouse in November 2020, she quickly realized she needed a strategy to leverage the platform for her business. "The first things I had to figure out," says Joy, "were what I was going to say to people about what I did and how I was going to be memorable." After watching several people throwing out different pitches based on the room they were in, Joy recognized the importance of consistency. From that point, she used the same introduction in every room. "My name is Joy Pittman, and I'm the Olivia Pope of HR. I'm on a mission to help black female entrepreneurs stop being overworked and underpaid CEOs of their own businesses."

Beyond her introduction, Joy had a strategy for how and where she showed up. In the beginning, she often spent time in smaller rooms where the topics interested her and were relevant to her business. Whenever she raised her hand to speak in those rooms, she focused on sharing value. She didn't pitch her services or herself. Instead, she let her value-add speak for itself.

It didn't take long for other Clubhouse users in larger rooms to recognize Joy when she showed up. Within a month, Joy had more than one thousand followers on Clubhouse. She would go into rooms started by people she followed, and someone would recognize her and shout her out as the HR expert who had dropped gems in another room. With that credibility, Joy started hosting her own rooms and started her own club, Hire Like a Boss. From her stage, she continues to give tons of value and finally talks about her offers. Joy also invites her clients to join her onstage to share what it's like to work with her and the kinds of results they've gotten. As a result of these strategies, Joy has attracted new clients to her business, including one who booked a $60,000 package.

Adriane Simpson

WHAT IS CLUBHOUSE, REALLY?

Every few years, a new social media platform seems to come out of nowhere and catch everyone's attention. Some start off with a lot of buzz, only to quickly disappear. Some find a niche audience that can sustain them for years but fail to make an impact on the larger culture. And then there are the platforms that transform the way we interact online. They offer the marketplace something we never knew we wanted until it showed up on our phones and computers and tablets. They find favor with the right early adopters and influencers, who attract enough people to build momentum. These are the platforms that change the game.

Clubhouse is one of those game-changer apps. Launched at the start of the COVID-19 pandemic, in March of 2020, it rapidly grew from tech geek hangout spot to the place to be—if you could get an invite. The app found its perfect audience of people spending even more time on their devices while they worked from home. Many people who might have overlooked it under normal circumstances were more than willing to give it a try in the middle of pandemic lockdowns.

As the pandemic continued and more people shared their invites, Clubhouse grew from 1500 members in

May 2020 to 10 million by February 2021.[1] It became the place to show up and be heard for everyone from celebrities to venture capitalists, from online entrepreneurs to CEOs of major companies. We've seen participation from rapper Meek Mill, actress and comedian Tiffany Haddish, CEO of Tesla and SpaceX, Elon Musk, talent manager and famous father Matthew Knowles, a VP of Engineering at LinkedIn and Amazon hiring managers, author and speaker Luvvie Ajayi, and leaders in the diversity and inclusion space like Keya Grant, director of supplier inclusion for Papa John's International.

Clubhouse is an audio-only app, where people meet to have conversations about topics of interest. There are no recordings, no comments, and no likes, loves, or sad faces. Since there's no video or images, except profile pics, Clubhouse is a "come as you are" opportunity to connect in real time. In a season of Zoom burnout, fake backgrounds, and looking your best from the waist up, many users find it refreshing to connect and communicate without all the window dressing. You could be sitting at your desk or lying in your bed. You could be wearing a suit and tie or a wrap dress, or much more likely, sweats or pajamas. No one knows, and no one cares. What counts on Clubhouse is what you have to say—and who you've connected with on the app and elsewhere. It's unique. It's powerful. And it's addicting.

As of now, Clubhouse is an invite-only app available only to iOS users. This means to join the network you have to: 1) know someone willing to extend you an invite and 2) be a user of Apple mobile products (an iPhone or an iPad). But if you're an Android user, don't despair. Clubhouse CEO Paul Davidson has said the platform will eventually be open to everyone, like all the major social media platforms, and currently has an Android app in development. That means Clubhouse will eventually extend to Android and other operating systems—if it hasn't already by the time you read this—making it accessible to almost anyone with a smartphone or tablet.

In the meantime, the app still has a certain amount of exclusivity. That sense of scarcity and those feelings of FOMO just make it more appealing to people waiting to get in. More and more, they're actively seeking invites to join. Some people have gone so far as to buy and sell invites on sites like Etsy and eBay, not a move I advise since you'll be permanently connected to the person who transacts with you to buy or sell that invite.

People join Clubhouse for all sorts of reasons. At any given time, you can drop in on conversations about dating and relationships, climate change, vegan lifestyles, corporate life, entrepreneurship, bitcoin, books, music, or film. It can be a fun place to hang out, connect with people all over the world, and explore new ideas. However, Clubhouse can do so much more than entertain you. If you're a busy professional with your eyes open for the next opportunity to advance your career or you have an urgent need to find a new job sooner rather than later, Clubhouse can help you achieve those goals. If you're an entrepreneur, and you need to drive more sales, increase your brand visibility, and grow your bottom line, Clubhouse is still the right place to be. While many people may be there to pass the time, many others are there to do business, and you can use the social media platform to accelerate your success.

WHY YOU SHOULD BE ON CLUBHOUSE ASAP

If you're like most professionals and entrepreneurs, you probably didn't jump on Snapchat or TikTok as soon as you heard about them. In fact, you might never have taken either of those apps seriously because you couldn't see how they might serve you. If you're busy running a business or climbing the corporate ladder, you may be looking at Clubhouse and wondering if it's worth the effort to get on yet one more social media platform. Simply put: *Yes, Clubhouse is absolutely worth your time.*

Used strategically, Clubhouse can help you accomplish almost any career or business goals you've set for yourself. It's a place to connect with recruiters from top companies, hiring managers from companies of all sizes, and decision makers in a wide variety of industries. As a business owner, it's a place where you can quickly grow your email list or develop warm leads. You can nurture clients, find funding, and even sell products through your engagement on Clubhouse. You can use the app to grow your following on other social media platforms and create a community for your followers or your peers. Whatever your goals are, Clubhouse can help you achieve them.

POTENTIAL PITFALLS AND HOW TO AVOID THEM

As with any new social media platform, it's easy to fall into the abyss and waste a lot of time on Clubhouse. There's almost always an interesting conversation you can participate in, some of which last for hours. It's easy to convince yourself that you're working or networking when you're really just wandering aimlessly from one Clubhouse room to the next. The biggest mistake users make on Clubhouse is the same mistake they make on other social media platforms. They don't have a purpose. Getting clear about your objectives will help you use Clubhouse as a tool rather than a distraction.

There are other Clubhouse pitfalls that can trip you up, but they're all easily overcome if you follow the steps in this book. In the following pages, you'll get my strategies to leverage Clubhouse for your professional success. I lay out specific steps you can implement to make the most of your time on the platform. Many of these are must-dos for everyone, regardless of your goals. I also share strategies you can choose from based on which are most aligned with your objectives. It's perfectly fine to be social on Clubhouse—that's what it's made for—but these steps will help you also be intentional with the time you spend there.

chapter 2
GET COMFORTABLE ON CLUBHOUSE

Business owner LaTaunya Johnson-Weaver (@restwell) bounced in and out of different rooms with widely varying topics of discussion when she first joined Clubhouse. However, she soon found a couple of rooms hosted by Amazon store experts and stopped in to glean some of their knowledge. Within a week, LaTaunya had set up her Amazon store and moved surplus merchandise that had been sitting in her warehouse to the tune of $2500 in sales. For her, it was just the beginning of leveraging Clubhouse to increase her bottom line. Since then, she has gotten comfortable on the app and begun moderating rooms for other speakers and expanding her network by connecting with experts in different industries.

DJ Kimani Smith (@djkimani) has only been on Clubhouse for a few months, but his time there has already proven fruitful. The site has allowed him to network with people across the music industry, including artists whose work he admires as a fan, and with other DJs. Kimani belongs to a Clubhouse club for DJs, where members discuss new artists to watch, current trends, and the latest in deejaying equipment.

"Recently I've been able to talk to some legendary people that I've met before but just haven't spoken to in a long time," says Kimani. "It was good to reconnect not only on a personal level but professionally as well." Kimani has quickly gotten up to speed on Clubhouse, and he's using the platform to deepen his knowledge of his industry, build relationships, and secure new opportunities.

Just like LaTaunya, Kimani has found the right balance for the time he spends on Clubhouse. He's taken the time to survey the landscape, get to know how things work, and find his people. That all started with understanding how the app works and making the most of those features. If you're not on Clubhouse yet, I recommend you read through this chapter before you jump on the app. If you're already active on the app, I still suggest you don't skip this chapter. You'll find some best practices that can help you maximize your time there.

Adriane Simpson

HOW TO GET ON CLUBHOUSE

Right now, Clubhouse is still invite-only, though this could change at any time. If you don't know anyone who can give you an invite, you can get on the Clubhouse waiting list. That way, you'll reserve your Clubhouse username, and when someone you know on Clubhouse has invites to share, they'll see you're waiting for access and can invite you to join. The best way to get an invite, if you haven't received one yet, is to let your friends or colleagues know you're interested. When they talk about Clubhouse, let them know you'd love to join them and support them there and make sure they have your phone number, which they'll need to send you the invite.

Download the Clubhouse app on your phone or tablet, reserve your username, and request access. This will save your username for you and essentially put you on a waiting list until someone you know sends you an invite. When that happens, you'll receive a notification to log in and join Clubhouse.

If you don't have an iOS device, you still have some options. You can download the Clubhouse app on a friend's Apple device and reserve your username there. Then, when you get an iOS device or when Clubhouse becomes available for other operating systems, such as Android, you'll already have your chosen username to sign up with. However, if you receive an invite, I don't suggest you log in to Clubhouse on anyone else's device. If the other person has shared their contacts with Clubhouse, those contacts may become associated with your account.

Ideally, the person who invited you to Clubhouse should onboard you. They should welcome you onto the app and walk you through how it works. When you first join, people who have your number in their contacts, including the person who invited you, will receive a notification letting them know you joined and asking if they have a moment to welcome you in. If they choose to do so, they'll be taken to a private room and you'll be notified to join them there. This is an opportunity for that person to give you the rundown on Clubhouse.

In that private room, the two of you can talk to each other without interruption, and they can share with you how to maneuver around the app and explain the best practices and social mores of this community. The community guidelines for Clubhouse are different from most other social media platforms, so don't depend on the person who invited you to explain everything. Review the guidelines for yourself. (The guidelines can be found under settings. Click the gear icon on your profile page and scroll down.)

Keep in mind the person who invites you to join Clubhouse is forever linked to you. Your behavior on Clubhouse affects their standing there. To put it plainly, if you get kicked off the app for violating the conditions of use, so do they. Most people reading this book will never come close to crossing that line, but it's worth being aware of those consequences. Common courtesy and respect for others will almost always keep you from breaking most of the rules or violating most policies. One rule everyone should be aware of is that you cannot record, transcribe, or reproduce a Clubhouse room without prior permission.

Unfortunately, not enough people are taking advantage of the opportunity to welcome new members into Clubhouse, so many users are left to wander the hallway (Clubhouse speak for the main feed) on their own and figure things out. Fortunately, the layout is fairly simple, but if you want more direction, you can usually find a "Welcome to the Clubhouse" room, in which the speakers will walk you through the ins and outs of the app. At the moment, there's one running every morning.

For your first week on Clubhouse, your profile will display a party hat icon. This lets other members know you're a newbie so they can welcome you and give you some grace as you find your way around. Take advantage of this time and pop into rooms while you're still wearing the party hat. It's an easy and unobtrusive way to start friendly conversations and get a little extra attention from the veterans. Once you're comfortable on Clubhouse, make sure you take time to welcome newcomers too.

YOUR CLUBHOUSE PROFILE

I originally signed up to Clubhouse using my name, Adriane Simpson, as my username, but I soon changed it to reflect my business name. My business is The LinkedIn Pros, and my Clubhouse username is now @thelinkedinpro. I had to commit when I made that decision because Clubhouse only allows users to change their username once. In my profile, my name still appears as Adriane Simpson, so people can still find me by searching for my name.

Clubhouse encourages people to use their real names in their profile, and this is usually the best option when you're looking to use the app to grow your professional network, advance your career, or expand your business. If you can get it, it's usually best to use your real name as your username too. Another option is to use your business name or some combination of the two as your username.

Rather than type your profile bio in the Clubhouse app, I suggest you type it in the Notes app and then copy and paste it to Clubhouse. If you view my profile, you'll notice I have emojis—not smiley faces or shrugs, but relevant icons—in my bio. This breaks up the text, making it easier to read and making it easier for followers to quickly find specific information about me. For example, I have a telephone next to the call to action "Schedule time with me." I have a chain-link next to URLs. You can't find these emojis on Clubhouse, but it's easy to write your profile description in Notes and then paste it in Clubhouse.

Keep your most important bio details "above the fold" or at the top of your bio where people will see that information even if they don't scroll down to keep reading. If you want people to know you're a personal stylist or a public speaker or that your business creates corporate gift baskets or natural haircare products, put this information at the top of your bio. In fact, the most important information should appear in the first three lines. This is the information people will see in your abbreviated bio when they click on your profile picture while you're in a room together. Then, include other details like what you want people to do to connect with you further, who you work with, or what kinds of connections you're looking to make. Finally, you can include personal details that might resonate with people you want to connect with, including organizations you're active in or the name of your alma mater.

You should also include your Twitter and Instagram handles in your bio if you use these platforms. These will be the only live hyperlinks in your bio. For many people, tapping your Twitter or IG will be the fastest way to connect with you outside of Clubhouse, so give them that opportunity. As you create or join clubs, the icons for those clubs will appear at the bottom of your profile page.

When you create your bio, make sure you use keywords from your profession and your industry. Any words you use in your bio will be searchable by other Clubhouse users. For example, if your bio says, "owner of the best SAT tutoring service in the world," your name will come up when someone searches for "SAT tutoring service." Interestingly, people can also search for people and clubs by emojis, so choose relevant emojis for your profile.

Visit bit.ly/ClubhouseQuickStart to download my free checklist, "Create an Eye-Catching Clubhouse Profile," and make sure you're set up for success on Clubhouse.

WHO TO FOLLOW

When you first get on Clubhouse, it can be tempting to follow all the people you know because there's comfort in the familiar. It can also be tempting to follow the big names in your industry or in industries you find interesting or to jump on the celebrity bandwagon. As of right now, and not at all surprisingly, Tiffany Haddish has 4.1 million Clubhouse followers. Mark Zuckerberg has 1.2 million. There's nothing wrong with following those people, but you'll want to diversify the people you follow beyond the big names.

The app will recommend people for you to follow based on your contacts, should you choose to share them with Clubhouse, and some of the interests you choose. When you tap on the search icon (the usual magnifying glass), you'll land on the Explore page, where you can search for people or interest-based clubs to follow. There, you'll find a suggested "People to Follow," and you can decide if you want to follow any of these people. In the next section of the page, you'll see "Find Conversations About..." with several categories you can explore, which will lead you to clubs and people you might want to follow. Explore this area and decide which people, clubs, and interests are in alignment with how you plan to use Clubhouse. Choose wisely.

Follow people who are speaking about subjects you're curious about or interested in—and whose expertise is relevant to your goals— to get started. Clubhouse will notify you when they're speaking in a room. Next, search for clubs that interest you and where you might find people with similar or complementary goals. You want to listen, learn, and enjoy your time on Clubhouse, but you don't want it to take up hours of your time every day. Focus on maximizing your time on the app by following the people most in alignment with what you want to learn, the kinds of connections you want to make, and your business or professional goals.

The same general principle applies to selecting your interests. If you're into cycling and international travel but don't really want to use Clubhouse to learn more about those activities, don't search those interests. It's all too easy to get caught up in interesting conversations about your hobbies, which can distract you from your concrete goals. Instead, stay focused on what you want to get out of Clubhouse. Choose interests in alignment with those goals.

Visit bit.ly/ClubhouseQuickStart to download my free process map, "Your Clubhouse Follower Strategy," and quickly figure out who to follow and who to pass by on Clubhouse.

INVITES

You'll get on Clubhouse because someone invites you, and once you're there, you'll have the opportunity to invite other people. Click on the envelope icon at the top of the hallway (the main feed), and you'll see how many invites you have available. Initially, Clubhouse required users to grant the app access to their phone's contacts. Because of privacy concerns, this is no longer a requirement. If you've given Clubhouse access to your contacts, you'll see a list of names you recognize on this screen. You can invite any one of your contacts by clicking the blue Invite button and customizing the message you send to them. If you choose not to share your contacts with the app, you can manually type in a contact's phone number to send them an invite.

But wait! Before you invite anyone to join Clubhouse, ask yourself how well you know this person. If you click on your profile picture and scroll down your profile page, you'll see the date you joined and "Nominated by." The person who nominated you is forever attached to your profile, and anyone you invite will be tied to you as well. In fact, if someone you invite violates the Clubhouse rules and is kicked off the app, you too will be removed from Clubhouse. I've seen people offer their invites to strangers on social media, and it makes me believe they're either unaware of or unconcerned about the possibility of losing access to the platform. Use discretion as you dole out your invites. One person's poor choice could cost you access to this valuable community.

As you use Clubhouse more, you'll notice you have more invites to extend. Clicking on the envelope icon at the top of the hallway will also show you how many invites you've extended that are still pending and how many you have left. The way invites are handed out to users can change at any time, so there's no predicting how many you'll have to give, but using them can help you grow your Clubhouse community and add more followers. I've even seen invites used as prizes for contest giveaways, which, because of that permanent connection, may or may not be a good idea.

Adriane Simpson

WELCOMING NEW USERS

When a new user joins Clubhouse, people who have the user's phone number in their contacts receive a notification that says, "Jane Doe just signed up for Clubhouse. Free to welcome them in?" If you have the opportunity to welcome the people you've invited or other people in your network to Clubhouse and help them get up to speed on the app, you should definitely do it. It's an easy courtesy to extend, and they'll likely appreciate it. You'll be taken to a private room (See below.) and that person will be invited to join you. There you can give them the rundown of how Clubhouse works. Just know that everyone isn't aware of this option. They may not show up to the private room you've created simply because they don't understand how the process works.

ROOMS

A room is a conversation started by a Clubhouse user to discuss a particular subject. Your objective is to get in the right rooms to listen to, engage in, and eventually host the right conversations. When you log in to Clubhouse, you'll see recommended rooms based on who you follow and any interests you've selected. As you participate more on the app, the algorithm will make better recommendations about what you may be interested in. As you choose more and more varied interests, you'll be notified about or shown more rooms.

Once you join a room, take the time to listen and get a feel for the conversation. If the discussion seems valuable to you, then you might choose to stay for as long as you can. If you think someone you're connected with can benefit from the information being shared, you can ping them by tapping the plus button at the bottom of the screen while you're in the room. Click on that person's image, and if their notifications are on, they'll be notified that you invited them to the room. They can choose to join you or not. You're certainly not required to hang out until the room closes as some rooms can last for hours. To leave, simply tap "Leave quietly" at the bottom of your screen.

Rooms are divided into three sections. The first section is made up of speakers, including the host who started the room. In this section, you'll see at least one speaker whose profile picture is outlined in gray. This person has their mic open. In other words, they have the ability to speak and aren't muted. In the same section, you may see several people whose profile picture is accompanied by a microphone icon with a slash through it. These people are onstage and have permission to speak but are currently muted.

The second section of a room is made up of people who aren't onstage, but who are followed by the speakers. The last group consists of "others in the room," people who have come to listen, learn, and ask questions, but who don't fit in either of the first two groups. Anyone in the audience can tap the raised-hand icon to request the chance to speak, but not all rooms will provide an opportunity for audience members to speak up or ask questions.

If you're in a room and hear one of the speakers refer to PTR, or pull to refresh, they're asking you to refresh your screen. To do this, simply hold down the screen at the top of the room and pull down, and the room will refresh. Speakers will sometimes ask you to do this when they've changed their profile picture for whatever reason. You can quickly change your own profile picture, even while you're in a room, by pressing and holding your profile picture. This will open a window for you to choose a new photo.

THE STAGE

In any Clubhouse room, you'll see at the top of the screen the people who are on stage. If they have a green and white asterisk icon next to their names, they're also moderators for the room. This includes the person who started the room and anyone else they've made a moderator. Moderators are the only people in the room who can invite people to join the speakers onstage, mute and unmute speakers, or turn off hand raising. The other speakers in the room can contribute to the conversation, but they can't control who's onstage or who can speak.

If you're in a room and are either invited onstage or have raised your hand to make a comment or ask a question, moderators can bring you up for a period of time and then remove you from the stage when you're done. As I'll remind you more than once, this is a chance to show up as the authentic you. You want people to get to know you, not your representative, but naturally, you also want to put your best foot forward. Show up as the professional you, but don't overthink it.

If you're invited in advance to speak in a room hosted by someone else, take some time to prepare the points you'll want to cover. Once you get there, thank the host for having you, stay engaged, allow other speakers to have their say, and even when you disagree with a speaker or audience member, keep the conversation civil and professional. If you raise your hand in the audience and are brought onstage, once again, thank the host for allowing you the opportunity to ask your question or share your comment. Make sure what you have to say is relevant and contributes to the conversation. Be aware of the rhythm of the conversation and give the speakers a chance to respond to your input. And know when to wrap it up. Even if you're only onstage for just a few minutes, if you add value, that time will often garner you more followers and more credibility.

In some rooms, you may notice the speakers' microphone icons flickering while someone else is speaking. This is a way for speakers to applaud whoever is speaking at the time. They click the microphone on and off to show their agreement or appreciation. If you're in a room where this is a practice, you can do this onstage too by tapping your microphone icon. But don't do it if you have background noise that can interrupt the speaker.

If you haven't started on Clubhouse yet and you're just reading the ins and outs, it can all seem like a lot. Fortunately, the creators of Clubhouse have done a great job giving us a fairly simple, user-friendly interface. Don't be intimidated. The fastest way to master this app is to use it regularly. Dive in, find your way around, and make yourself comfortable so you can start leveraging Clubhouse to meet your goals.

chapter 3
BUT FIRST, A NECESSARY DETOUR TO LINKEDIN

When a recruiter from Amazon Web Services scheduled a room on Clubhouse, she posted the following on LinkedIn: "Join us today to meet and ask questions of recruiters from across Amazon – we are HIRING!!" For the prepared candidate, this kind of Q&A session provides the perfect opportunity to show up and get inside information or even talk yourself one step closer to a new job. This user collaboration between LinkedIn and Clubhouse is a complete disruption of the conventional recruiting and hiring process. As more companies recognize the ability to connect directly and start a conversation with the talent pool on Clubhouse, I expect to see similar rooms started every day by companies small and large.

The Amazon recruiter wisely promoted her Clubhouse room on LinkedIn, where many people actively seek work and took the conversation to Clubhouse where she could have a dynamic discussion with potential candidates. In a later chapter, I'll more specifically describe why LinkedIn and Clubhouse are perfect complements to each other. For now, know this. When you're actively looking for employment, many hiring managers and recruiters will check out your LinkedIn profile. If you don't have one or its incomplete or underwhelming, they won't take you seriously as a candidate. Instead, they'll focus on the person who has a robust and relevant LinkedIn presence because that presence allows them to get to know the candidate better. The same applies to entrepreneurs looking to secure contracts, attract more clients, and start strategic partnerships. Many of those people will check you out on LinkedIn to get a feel for how serious you are about your business. If they can't find much about you, they're likely to move on to someone else.

If you follow the process I lay out in this book, in the way I lay it out, you can expect to get results on

Clubhouse. However, you can't implement these strategies fully without tapping into another resource you've got right at your fingertips. Whatever you feel about LinkedIn, stick with me and know this detour is integral to creating the kind of success you want to have on Clubhouse—not just getting more followers or speaking on more stages, but achieving your specific and measurable professional goals.

I suggest you implement as much of this chapter as you possibly can while you're reading through it. That way, you won't miss any details or have a chance to procrastinate. Don't worry. I promise you we're coming back to Clubhouse in the very next chapter.

If you happen to think LinkedIn is boring or you rarely use it because you never know what to post there, you're not alone in your opinion or your experience. I've heard people liken LinkedIn to "church" or "a black hole." Their point is that it feels stuffy, overly formal, and not very social to them. Their expectations have been set by platforms like Facebook and Instagram, where personal posts tend to outweigh business posts. They're accustomed to cat videos and family pictures mixed in with business posts and ads. LinkedIn, on the other hand, is designed to be a professional social networking site, but I have good news. Professional doesn't have to equal boring, and you don't have to spend hours every day on LinkedIn to get results.

With over 720 million users worldwide and more than 170 million in the United States, there's absolutely someone, or more likely many people, on LinkedIn who can help you achieve your professional goals. If you think this site is just for older people, think again. Millennials comprise thirty-eight percent of users. This site is for anyone who's serious about advancing their career or growing their business regardless of age, gender, or geography.[2]

Eighty-seven percent of recruiters looking to fill roles regularly use LinkedIn.[3] If you're looking for a new job opportunity, you absolutely need to be active on this platform. And for those of us who own our own businesses, the opportunities available on LinkedIn are just as impressive. Event planners search the site to book speakers for conferences and seminars. Business owners shop for professional service providers and look for suppliers and employees, and investors research business owners on the site. As an entrepreneur, LinkedIn can help you find team members, strategic partners, customers and clients, and more.

If you're already present and active on LinkedIn, this chapter will give you a chance to review some basic best practices to make sure you're set up to make the most of your LinkedIn presence. And if you've avoided LinkedIn or you created your profile years ago and left it to gather dust, don't worry. I'll walk you through some simple steps to get started, set up or refresh your LinkedIn presence, and prepare to use the site as your secret weapon to maximize your time on Clubhouse. Trust the process. You've got nothing to lose and everything to gain.

GET ON LINKEDIN

Don't let the site's reputation intimidate you. LinkedIn is a social media platform open to anyone who wants to join. It's accessible regardless of whether you're on a Mac or PC, an Android tablet, Windows tablet, iPad, or any smartphone. To create your account, download the app on your phone or tablet, or visit LinkedIn.com on your computer. Tap "Join Now," and follow the simple prompts to create your account. It's that simple.

YOUR LINKEDIN PROFILE

Before you start connecting with people on LinkedIn, it's important to create a profile with elements that will appeal to the people already in your professional network and those you want to connect with in the future. This is a place to show your authentic self, of course, but always in a professional manner. Users visit this site to conduct business of various kinds, and it's important to project an image of yourself as someone who understands the purpose of the site. Don't skimp or get lazy on this essential step. It shouldn't take you more than a few hours to create a comprehensive and appealing profile. Going forward, periodic updates will only take you a few minutes.

Before you update your profile take the time to do a little research. If you're looking for job opportunities, search for other people in your industry, in similar positions, and in positions you might want. If you're a small business owner, look for people who own similar businesses or offer similar services. Choose people who have large networks and comprehensive profiles. If you know who the top players are in your field, include them in your search. Make a list of the keywords they have in common, and when they apply, use these words in your profile.

Use all the available real estate LinkedIn gives you including:

1. Your name
2. Profile picture
3. Headline
4. Current position
5. Education
6. Geographic location
7. Branded URL
8. Contact information
9. About (Your positioning statement)
10. Skills and endorsements
11. Recommendations
12. Accomplishments

YOUR NAME

To start, use your real name for your LinkedIn profile. This isn't the place for nicknames or even your business name. (You can create a business page for your business.) People on LinkedIn want to know exactly who they're interacting with, considering doing business with, and considering for job placements. Besides your name, you should also include the abbreviations for specific certificates or degrees, like CPA, MD, JD, PMP, MBA, or the like. My LinkedIn username is Adriane Simpson, PMP,

MBA, LSSGB. At a glance, recruiters, business owners, and potential clients can see some of the qualifications that separate me from other people in my field. (Note: If you don't yet have any letters to drop behind your name, don't let that stop you from using LinkedIn. They're not a requirement for success on this platform.)

On the mobile app, you can also record the correct pronunciation of your name. If your name has an unusual spelling or people often mispronounce it, consider taking advantage of this function. Some people will be more comfortable reaching out to you if they know how to say your name, so make it easy for them.

PROFILE PICTURE

When choosing your profile picture, make sure it represents you as a professional. Even if your industry is a more creative or casual one, your picture should reflect a level of seriousness about what you do. If you're a professional clown, then you may want to appear in your clown makeup, but for most of us, a friendly-looking headshot with a professional appearance is the best choice. Make sure the photo is bright, crisp, and clear with a solid, uncluttered background.

Adriane Simpson

HEADLINE

Your headline should include the roles you want to be associated with in searches. As a job seeker, you can list your current role and roles you've held in the past. As a small business owner, you can list the work you do and for which people are likely to be searching. Rather than call herself CEO in her headline, an entrepreneur might have a headline that reads: Cyber Security | Remediation Services | Security Testing. She's CEO of her company, but she doesn't want to be found in searches for CEOs. She wants potential customers who need help with cyber security to find her.

LinkedIn is a huge search engine, and like all search engines, it has its own set of rules. For instance, it doesn't recognize commas between words in your headline. Rather than use commas, list your roles or services by separating each one with a divider (|). This way, the search engine will recognize them as individual keywords.

Leave information that won't help you come up in relevant searches out of your headline. Many people include the name of the company they work for here, but it's not helpful because people don't typically use company names when they're searching for someone to hire, work with, or buy from on this site. Don't include your company name in your headline.

CURRENT POSITION

Whether you own your business or work for someone else, this is the place to list both your role and the company name. The business name will appear on your profile page, near your headline.

EDUCATION

Add the names of the institutions from which you've received degrees or where you're in the process of pursuing a degree. Only the name of the institution will appear above the fold on your profile page. Further down on the page, you'll have the opportunity to include more information about your educational background, including your degree(s), field(s) of study, and the start and end dates of your attendance at each institution. I recommend you fill in everything except the dates. They don't add any value and can actually work against you. If you've recently graduated, people may see you as inexperienced. If you graduated some time ago, some people will judge you as too old. Ageism is real. Don't give anyone reason to hold your perceived age against you before they get to know you.

GEOGRAPHIC LOCATION

LinkedIn allows you to either let the app choose your current location or enter a zip code for your location. In this age of remote work, it might seem like your location is irrelevant, but on this site, it makes a difference. If you're focused on advancing your career with a job search, keep in mind that many recruiters will search for candidates based on location. If you're a small business owner, know that many of your clients, customers, and potential partners may be searching by location as well. While it may feel limiting, you may be left out of search results if you don't include a location on your profile.

PROFILE URL

Take advantage of the opportunity to personalize the URL associated with your LinkedIn profile. You may not be able to get your name, but you can get some variation of it. My LinkedIn URL is linkedin.com/in/adrianesimpson1913. Importantly, it has my name, but it also has the founding year of my sorority, Delta Sigma Theta Sorority, Inc. To many people, that date will have no meaning. But to people familiar with or affiliated with the organization, it's a moment of instant connection. Right away, they know something more about me.

To create your branded URL, go in to edit your LinkedIn profile. Scroll down to edit your contact info, and follow the prompts to create your profile URL. As LinkedIn evolves, you may find this option has moved to another spot, but I don't expect it to ever go away. Customize your URL and when you want to share your LinkedIn profile, you'll be able to do so easily.

CONTACT INFORMATION

Make it as easy as possible for people who might want to work with you, buy from you, hire you, or partner with you to get in touch with you outside of LinkedIn. Use your best email address here, and make sure your professionalism extends to that email address. If you've still got the email address you created in high school, and it screams teenager, create a new one and use it here. If you're open to contact by phone, include your phone number, and if you're a business owner, include your company website.

ABOUT (YOUR POSITIONING STATEMENT)

Think of this section as your positioning statement. This is your chance to position yourself as you wish to be perceived by anyone who comes across your LinkedIn profile. If you have a small business, this section should make a clear promise about what you deliver to your target market. As a corporate professional, your positioning statement should explain, at a high level, what you do well and how your skills can serve an employer. Even though you want to use common keywords here, you should also make sure your "About" section separates you from the competition in your field.

EXPERIENCE

Consider the "Experience" section of your LinkedIn profile a high-level view of your resume. You don't need to cram your entire resume into this section. Instead, you'll include each company name, job title, and a brief description of your job duties. Some people use bullet points for this section, but I've found it more effective to write in short paragraphs. Limit your experience here to the last fifteen years or so of your career.

This section is important for two reasons. First, when you come up in searches, people who are considering hiring you or working with you will often dive into this section to get more insight about your practical experience. Second, LinkedIn will periodically suggest connections to you based on the places you've worked. This can help you build your network in an organic way.

SKILLS AND ENDORSEMENTS

Your skills are the things you know how to do. They're also things people may be searching for on LinkedIn. To increase the chances that some of those searches lead to you, list your relevant skills in this section. Some coaches will suggest you pack this section with as many skills as possible, but I've found it more effective to focus on no more than ten skills here. It's more important to be perceived as great at a few important things than someone whose knowledge and ability are spread thin.

Your LinkedIn connections can also endorse you for one or more of these skills. In fact, some of your connections may endorse you for skills you haven't even listed for yourself. In those cases, you can decide to add the pending endorsement to your profile or ignore it. The value of these endorsements is hard to quantify, but if the skill is relevant to your LinkedIn goals, then an endorsement can't hurt.

LinkedIn has also added skills quizzes as an option for users. Essentially, users go through a multiple-choice quiz to determine their level of knowledge and proficiency in specific skillsets. This could be beneficial for you if you don't yet have deep experience, certifications, or formal education in a particular area. A skill quiz can demonstrate to others that you've developed mastery in that area.

RECOMMENDATIONS

Anyone connected to you can visit your LinkedIn profile and write you a recommendation. However, LinkedIn won't allow anyone to comment on your profile, in any way, without your permission. If someone writes you a recommendation, it will only appear on your profile after you accept it. This is an important safeguard, protecting LinkedIn users from the kind of trolls who run rampant on many social media platforms.

Recommendations can be particularly valuable because the writer has a chance to express *why* they're recommending you. They can write in detail about their experience working with you, the role you played in helping them achieve their goals, and why other people should work with you. In this section, tap on "Ask for a recommendation" to request a recommendation from any of your connections. Of course, you'll want to choose people with whom you've had or currently enjoy a successful working relationship and who know you well enough to write about your professional performance.

ACCOMPLISHMENTS

Use this section to share achievements that help you stand out from other people in your role or your industry. You'll have the option to include publications, patents, courses, projects, honors and awards, test scores, languages, and organizations. One of my clients was on the team that developed a new technology, which the company then patented. The company owns the patent, but his is one of the names on it, and he has listed that accomplishment on his LinkedIn profile. Don't be shy about sharing what you've done. List your relevant accomplishments here.

Like all the popular social media sites, LinkedIn regularly makes changes to improve your user experience. Visit the site regularly—at least once a week—to stay on top of and take advantage of any innovations that allow you to better position yourself, get more visibility, or make connections more efficiently and effectively. As you learn new skills, get certifications, change positions, or have new accomplishments to share, update your profile accordingly.

Yes, there are several sections to fill in, but this isn't complicated. This is all information you know about yourself. You may need to refer to your resume for details and dates, but it's worth taking the time to open that document and get the information that will make it easy for people to find you so they can work with you, hire you, buy from you, or connect with you. Take the time to fill out your profile as thoroughly as possible. And update it regularly. Nothing about social media is permanent. Social media is meant to evolve. You'll miss out on the full benefits of LinkedIn—or any other platform—if you allow your profile and presence to stagnate.

Visit bit.ly/ClubhouseQuickStart to download my free checklist, "Create an Eye-Catching LinkedIn Profile," and make sure you're set up for success on LinkedIn.

MAKING CONNECTIONS

Once you connect with a person on LinkedIn, you'll notice "1st" comes up next to their name. That means this person is your first-degree connection. In other words, you're directly connected with each other. Other profiles may appear in your searches as "2nd," which means you're not yet connected with each other but share at least one first-degree connection in common. Lastly, people noted as 3rd+ are connected to at least one of your second-degree connections.

One of the reasons so many people give up on LinkedIn before they see any results is a lack of strategy. I coach my clients to approach their LinkedIn connections with their goals in mind. When you're just getting started, the easiest step to take is to start with the familiar. Search for and connect with people you know on LinkedIn—people who have the kind of professional image you're happy to be associated with on this public platform.

Type a name in the search bar. Once you find that person, click on their profile, and then, tap "Connect." LinkedIn will give you a chance to customize your invitation to connect. You can always take time to do this, but this step isn't critical with people who know you well.

With your permission, LinkedIn will also access your contacts and suggest connections based on that data. This can be beneficial if your contact list contains current or former customers and clients or people you've met at in-person or online networking events. Building your number of connections before you reach out to new people is helpful for a couple of reasons. First, people who don't know you will take you more seriously if you already have some connections and will be more likely to accept your invitation to connect. Second, you'll be more likely to have a 2nd degree connection to some of the people you don't personally know but with whom you'll want to connect in your next round of invitations. Evidence of shared contacts will make many people more likely to accept your invitation.

If you've completed your profile, LinkedIn will also suggest people you might want to connect with based on information like where you work now or have worked in the past, schools you've attended, and organizations you're associated with. Remember your goal is to advance your career or grow your business, so use your discretion when you choose the people you add on LinkedIn.

Growing your connections beyond people you already know is where the real strategy comes in. Your goal will determine your strategy. If, for example, you're looking for a new job, I suggest you come up with a list of target companies in the city where you live or want to live and the industry or industries you're interested in. I can't emphasize enough how important it is to do your research and narrow down your targets. When I met my husband a zillion years ago, one of the first questions I asked him on our first date was: "Is Atlanta your forever home?" Fortunately, his answer was yes. You're not looking for dates on LinkedIn, but the point is that I was clear in my intentions and only "targeted" potential partners who met that important requirement. You should be just as intentional in targeting potential employers.

After I went through one of the four layoffs I experienced, I researched companies headquartered in

Atlanta because there was a high likelihood that they would have several job openings here in my city. I focused my search on those companies because it was important for me to stay in this location. I wasn't interested in jobs that might require me to relocate. If you're in a job search, define your priorities and target companies that match your priority list. Connect with: 1) people in jobs similar to the job you're seeking, 2) people at your target companies, 3) people in your target industry, 4) people whose professional achievements you admire, and 5) leaders in similar industries.

If you're a small business owner, your connection strategy will be informed by your short-term and long-term business goals. After connecting with friends and colleagues, I encourage my small business clients to look at their business goals to create their strategy. Based on those goals, people you connect with may include: 1) business owners in your industry, 2) business owners in complementary industries, 3) business owners in your city or town, 4) potential clients and customers, 5) potential suppliers, 6) potential vendors, 7) potential strategic partners, 8) potential investors, and 9) potential employees.

Any effective networking strategy starts with research, some of which will take place on LinkedIn.

Search for relevant keywords like the names of your target companies and the position you desire. Then take the time to view the profiles of some of the people who come up in your search. Make a connection when it makes sense for your goals.

Other research, you'll need to do outside of LinkedIn. Fortunately, you have the entire Internet at your fingertips. There's almost nothing you need to know that you can't find online if you invest a little time in searching for the right companies and people.

Sometimes, when you attempt to send an invitation to connect, LinkedIn will ask you to enter that person's email address. According to LinkedIn, this may happen for three reasons: 1) the user has requested only people who know their email address send invitations, 2) you've already sent an invitation to that user, or 3) "a number of recipients have clicked **I don't know [name]** after getting your invitations."[4]

If you get this message, it doesn't necessarily mean you've done something wrong. It could be that the person you want to connect with is filtering his or her connections to only connect with people they've already interacted with offline or on other platforms. In my experience, it's unlikely that too many people have reported to LinkedIn that they don't know you.

They'd first have to tap "Ignore" in response to your request and then take another step to indicate they don't know you. Most people won't bother, so don't let a request to enter the user's email address throw you off. If you don't have that information, just move on to your next invitation.

THE NUMBERS MATTER

It may take you some time to get there, but once you have more than five hundred connections on LinkedIn, the platform will display your number of connections as 500+. It doesn't make a difference if you have 501 connections or 5100, the number displayed on your profile will still be 500+. It's important to set a goal of hitting that milestone and to work towards it. Once you've hit that goal, you can work up to 1000 connections or more.

The number of connections matters for several reasons. LinkedIn-savvy professionals will take you much more seriously on the platform when they see your connections have reached 500+ because it demonstrates that you've invested the time to build your network. It identifies you as someone who's active on the platform and gives you more credibility than someone with a couple hundred connections. It also makes it much more likely that you'll appear in searches and that your content will be seen and shared. That being said, don't get so caught up in quantity that you forget about the quality of your connections.

While 500+ may seem like a big goal when you're just getting started, it doesn't have to overwhelm you. You won't have to do all the work because as you start to make connections and get active on the platform, you can expect other people to reach out and invite you to connect. You don't have to make all those connections overnight either. Let's break it down to more manageable numbers.

5 connections X 5 days = 25 connections per week
25 connections X 4 weeks = 100 connections per month
100 connections X 5 months = 500 connections

That means you only need to reach out to, on average, five people per day. Five months isn't a long time to build a network that can serve you for the length of your career. If your LinkedIn goals are more time sensitive, then double that number and invite ten people to connect each day. You get to decide how aggressively you'll build your network, and the only standard by which you need to measure is your own goal.

INVITING STRANGERS TO CONNECT

As we've already covered, some of the people you want to connect with will be completely unfamiliar with you. Inviting them to connect requires a little more finesse, but it's totally possible to make those connections happen. Quality connections don't typically happen with people who accept every invitation they get. You need to put in a little more effort to stand out in a crowded inbox.

If you have a solid profile, a LinkedIn member who shows up as your second-degree connection is likely to accept your invitation to connect even if they don't know you personally. They can see who you are and what you do, and they can tell you have some connections in common. However, it's always best practice to add a personal note to your invitation when connecting to someone you haven't met. This is especially important with a third-degree connection. This person is more like a second cousin twice removed. Your network ties aren't close enough for them to feel like they know you.

To improve your chances that they'll connect with you, personalize your invitation.

LinkedIn only gives you three hundred characters to write a personal note with your invitation to connect, but that's more than enough. Make sure you express why you're looking to connect with this specific person. This can be as simple as mentioning an interest, an organization, or colleagues you have in common.

I'm from the school of thought that teaches "Be a giver, not a taker," and that certainly applies here. Giving can be as simple as offering: "Please let me know if there's anyone in my network with whom I might connect you." There are simple ways to let the person know you've taken the time to get to know something about them and your shared interests, and that you're not just looking to sell them something or randomly connect with as many people as possible.

ACCEPTING CONNECTIONS

Just as you shouldn't invite random people to connect on LinkedIn, you shouldn't say yes to every request to connect with you. If you don't know the person requesting to connect, then consider their level of professionalism, their reputation, and how they comport themselves online and in the real world. If this is someone you'd associate with in a professional setting offline, then by all means, accept the invitation.

Assessing the quality of requests from people you don't know takes a little more due diligence, but it only takes a few minutes. Look at your level of connection and see who you may know in common. On LinkedIn, it's perfectly reasonable to judge people by the company they keep. If you have several connections in common or one or two shared connections who you know well and the person's profile is reasonably strong, it's probably a safe bet that this will be a quality connection for you.

When you get invitations to connect from complete strangers with whom you have no connections in common—and you will—pay attention to the details. Examine the profile to get to know this person a bit and to see what interests or experiences you may share. Look at the invitation. Did they send a personal note to explain why they want to connect? The reason should add value for both of you and should make sense. If, for example, the invitation reads, "I noticed you're a divorce coach and wanted to connect," when in actuality you're a private chef, this might be one you want to decline.

POSTING ON LINKEDIN

People often tell me they don't post on LinkedIn because they have no idea what to post on a platform they see as formal and stuffy. But here's the truth. Posting on LinkedIn is no more difficult than posting on any other platform. As long as your posts portray you in a professional manner, they can also be creative and should always be interesting. Just as you can on other social platforms, you can post articles, images, and video content.

While I recommend you build up to posting every day, everything you post doesn't have to be original content. You can also share articles and videos from other experts. I've created a tactical posting calendar for my career coaching and small business clients, so they always know what to post next. You can create the same kind of calendar for yourself by starting with your professional or entrepreneurial goals. Simply decide what kind of content can support those goals and map it out so that, each day, you know if you're posting your own content or shared content, video or something written and what topics you'll cover.

Visit bit.ly/ClubhouseQuickStart to download my free process map, "What to Post on LinkedIn and When," and make sure your LinkedIn presence positions you for success.

Adriane Simpson

HOW TO MAKE THE MOST OF LINKEDIN

I've created an entire system for leveraging LinkedIn, my Executive Success System, which I share with my coaching clients. The full extent of the system is beyond the scope of this book, but you don't need to implement the full system to leverage LinkedIn and Clubhouse together. Employ the best practices I've shared for getting started on LinkedIn and making connections, and you'll be more than halfway to making the most of both platforms.

To maintain your LinkedIn presence with a minimal investment of time:

1. Update your profile regularly, especially when you join new organizations, take on new positions, learn new skills, have new accomplishments to share, or add new offerings to your business.
2. Continue to grow your network on the platform by sending invitations to connect with people you meet or with whom you'd like to build a relationship.

3. Respond to messages and invitations to connect in a timely manner.
4. Set your posting schedule and stick to it.
5. Engage with other people's posts—like, comment, share—especially posts by people with whom you'd love to build a deeper relationship.

Maximizing your LinkedIn presence is essential to the Clubhouse strategy you're building here. Keep in mind that some of the Clubhouse users who see you onstage, converse with you in rooms, or follow you will check out your LinkedIn profile to make sure you're legit. Yes, they may also look at your tweets and your Instagram posts, but if they're serious about partnering with you in business, hiring you, or investing in you in some way, they're likely to examine your LinkedIn profile to make sure you're really the professional you say you are.

chapter 4
CREATE YOUR CLUBHOUSE STRATEGY

Fractional COO Sha' Cannon (@shacannoncoo) jumped into the unchartered Clubhouse waters with both feet. She shows up to host rooms in her own club five days a week and consistently shares other people's platforms six days a week when she moderates rooms for other influencers. Sha' also takes the time to visit other rooms where her audience hangs out. "I intentionally jump into small and large rooms to get on stage to tell people who I am and give value," says Sha'.

Her consistency has paid off with measurable results in three specific areas of her business. First, Sha' has seen her free discovery calls increase, leading to more paid strategy calls. Second, purchases of her passive income products have increased because she talks about the products as tools her audience can use to maximize the value of the information she shares from the stage. And third, her number of email list subscribers has grown because she has a link to her opt-in gift in her Clubhouse bio and refers to it often.

Sha' has seen her time on Clubhouse payoff in multiple ways because she's intentional about the time she spends there. While she enjoys it, she uses the app with specific, measurable goals in mind. When you create your own Clubhouse strategy, your goals will dictate how much time you invest in Clubhouse, what you offer there, and what value you choose to add.

While some of the Clubhouse user interface will inevitably change, the strategy you bring to your time on this app is evergreen, and it all starts with getting clear about your goals. When you join Clubhouse, intentionality and that clarity will drastically increase your chances of succeeding. Set measurable goals so you can periodically assess the return you're getting on your investment there. While your goals may be more "big picture" in the beginning, once you've gotten comfortable on Clubhouse, you can refine those goals and get even more specific.

SET SPECIFIC CLUBHOUSE GOALS

As short-term goals, you might set out to achieve any of the following:

- Add value to rooms for specific people you follow.
- Give more than you take by participating in a set number of rooms each week or each day.
- Grow your Clubhouse following to a specific number.
- Start a club and grow the membership to a specific number, thus positioning yourself as an expert in your niche.
- Grow your LinkedIn connections by connecting with people on Clubhouse and then inviting them to connect on LinkedIn, where you can message each other directly.
- Expand your following or connections on other social media platforms.

Any of these goals can help you develop a productive presence on Clubhouse and lay the foundation for your specific career and business goals.

As a professional in corporate America, your long-term goals might include:

- Grow your LinkedIn network.
- Connect with people in your current industry.
- Connect with people in industries where your skills are a good fit and where you might wish to work in the future.
- Connect with potential vendors or customers.
- Connect with hiring managers associated with your dream employers.

As a business owner, you might set goals like the following:

- Develop strategic partnerships.
- Connect with new affiliates who'll promote your products and services.
- Find wholesale opportunities.
- Cultivate relationships with ideal clients.
- Increase consultation calls to a specific number.
- Create a community around your philosophies and expertise.

- Increase your brand recognition.
- Grow your email list.

YOUR STRATEGY

Once you've set and prioritized your goals, it's time to figure out how you'll achieve them.

Answer the following questions as you develop your strategy:

- How often do you need to be on Clubhouse?
- In what capacity?
- Who else do you need to follow on Clubhouse?
- Who do you want to follow you?
- What interests do you need to follow?
- What clubs should you join?
- Who do you need to connect with to achieve your goals?
- Who needs to recognize your expertise so you can achieve those goals?
- What rooms do you want to start?
- How often do you need to start a room?
- How will you promote those rooms?

- Who do you want to connect with outside of Clubhouse?
- How will you connect with those people?
- What next step do you want your followers to take to connect with you or work with you in some capacity?
- How will you share your call to action with followers?

Visit bit.ly/ClubhouseQuickStart to download my free "Clubhouse Strategy Tracker" to easily plan and implement your Clubhouse monetization strategy.

chapter 5
SHARE YOUR EXPERTISE & STAND OUT

When publicist and owner of CNBetter Media Candace Ledbetter (@cnbettermedia) first joined Clubhouse in late October 2020, she had no idea what she'd find there. However, after popping into a few rooms, she quickly saw the app's potential. "Clubhouse was the best kept secret on social media, in my opinion," says Candace. "I saw it as a way for people to position their expertise in a way that would give them a platform, not only to showcase and share knowledge, but to also grow a qualified audience of leads and loyal followers that most would spend thousands of dollars in social ads to attract."

Candace has since made Clubhouse a mandatory element of the visibility and positioning strategies for her clients, and she's seen the results they've created. Her clients have landed speaking engagements and press interviews and successfully launched products and services all from their participation on Clubhouse.

SPEAK UP

Much of the value on Clubhouse comes from being heard, but you don't have to start your own room or club to have your voice heard on this platform. If you don't yet have many followers or you're just not ready to take that step (you will be sooner than you think), take the opportunity to speak up in other people's rooms. Well-positioned questions and comments will allow you to share your expertise while adding value to the room. When speakers ask for questions, you can raise your hand, and if they choose to bring you on the stage, you can participate in the discussion in a small but meaningful way.

Speakers who ask for questions and comments really do want to hear questions and comments. If you have a question, the odds are someone else in the room is seeking the same answers but is afraid to ask. Other people in the audience will appreciate that you spoke up. Your questions and comments can also serve the speakers by allowing them to cover something they may have missed in their talk or discussion, giving them insight into what their audience wants to know, and giving them another chance to display their expertise. You add value when you contribute to the conversation.

Be aware that if people in a room recognize your expertise or want to hear specifically from you for any reason, they may invite you to the stage. This happens to me fairly often, and while I always appreciate the gesture, I don't always accept the invitation. Sometimes, I'm just popping on Clubhouse for a minute and don't have time to join the stage. Other times, I prefer to listen and learn. In those instances, you always want to be gracious, but at the same time, avoid getting sucked in to jumping onstage when you haven't planned, really don't have time, and aren't necessarily serving your goals by doing so.

In the beginning, you might accept every invitation to speak, but keep in mind that this can be time consuming. If the room goes on for a couple of hours and you're on stage for a while, you may find it difficult to make a graceful exit. Of course, you might agree to speak to simply support a friend or colleague. That's part of the give and take of relationship-building, but stay focused on your goals and be cognizant of how much of the time you spend on the app is actually getting you closer to where you want to be.

When you add value to the conversation in a room, everyone benefits. The speaker gets more engagement. You get your questions answered and your voice is heard, and the other people in the room listen in on a more interesting conversation. In fact, when you contribute to the conversation in a valuable way, some of the people in the room may follow you, and often, the speakers will suggest that they do. However, if you don't gain any followers from your brief comment or question, don't worry too much about it. It can take repeated exposure for people to decide to follow you.

While it's natural to want to make an impression when you're speaking, hogging the mic is never the way to do so. We've all been in a seminar or workshop when someone from the audience takes the mic to ask a question and then tries to take over. They don't know when to stop talking. They tell their story as if we've all come to hear them speak, or they try to provoke the speakers onstage and draw them into unhelpful debate. Don't be that person on Clubhouse.

It can be exciting to have the chance to speak with people you admire or to have an audience for your questions and ideas. But a contribution turns to an annoyance when someone in the audience tries to hijack the room. It puts speakers and moderators in a bad position. It irritates the other people in the room, and it makes the hijacker look incredibly bad. Please don't be the hijacker.

When you're invited to speak on someone else's stage, be prepared to give the conversation your attention. Clubhouse speakers don't have visual cues to facilitate the conversation, so you have to actually listen to what's going on when you're sharing the stage with other people. You don't want to cut anyone off when they're still talking, but you don't want to leave dead air because no one knows when to speak either.

A good host will often call on different speakers to give their input in an orderly way. When they're onstage with multiple speakers, some speakers end their input by saying, "I'm John Doe, and I'm done speaking." This lets the next speaker know they can jump in. This culture is still developing, and people are still figuring out the best ways to keep conversations flowing.

Follow these common-sense rules for sharing someone else's stage:

1. Thank the speakers for allowing you to ask a question or join them onstage.

2. Stay on topic.
3. Don't monopolize someone else's stage or make the conversation all about you.

Break any of these three simple rules, and you may well damage your reputation, drastically reduce the likelihood that anyone in the room will follow you, and ruin any chance you have to make a real connection. Adhere to them, and you'll leave a positive impression on everyone in the room.

START A ROOM

Starting a room positions you as a leader, an expert, and an authority. Even if you're interviewing other experts and not sharing many of your own ideas, being on the stage lends you an air of credibility. Think about Oprah's career trajectory. For twenty-three seasons, she came into our living rooms as the host of *The Oprah Winfrey Show*. She interviewed experts (and regular people), and her viewers quickly came to view her as an expert in her own right. It worked for Oprah, so don't be afraid to share your stage with people who have a body of knowledge different from your own or to start interesting conversations with "regular" people.

As an acquaintance of mine recently learned when only a couple of people showed up to hear her speak, starting a room doesn't guarantee you an audience. She'd blocked her schedule in the middle of a workday to give this talk and was disappointed by the turnout. For the entire hour, she presented to and took questions from two people. It felt like a waste of her time and energy.

Your room is an event, and like any event, you need to do the legwork to get people to show up and participate. With the exception of celebrities and industry leaders with huge followings, a nearly (or totally) empty room can happen to anyone. Sometimes, it's simply a matter of poor scheduling. The speaker chooses a time when much of his or her potential audience is unavailable, and so, very few people attend. More often, however, a poor turnout is the result of not doing the groundwork before starting the room.

Starting rooms can help you grow your following, so don't hesitate to do it, but it's a good practice to understand the app and its functionality before you take that step. Once you feel comfortable with how things work, step up to be one of the small percentage of users who regularly starts rooms. The first step in building your potential audience for any room you'll start is to make connections on Clubhouse. Some of the people you follow will also follow you, and they'll be notified when you open a room. You can also get more followers by speaking up and going onstage in other people's rooms.

Put some thought into the subject matter for your room. Choose an engaging topic that will appeal to your audience. To do this, you'll need to know your audience and what interests them. If your topic is very niche, don't shy away from it. With a well-promoted niche topic, you can expect to have a smaller, but more targeted turnout. For example, while rooms about how to get venture capital for your business can have hundreds of people show up, a room about intermittent fasting for ethical vegans may have a smaller but more invested audience.

Give your room a clear and intriguing title, and then schedule the room in advance by clicking on the calendar icon at the top of the Clubhouse hallway. Then tap the calendar icon with a plus sign. This will take you to a screen where you can create a room, or "New Event," for a future date and time. You'll include the event name, the names of any co-hosts or guest speakers, the day and time, and a short description of your room. Hit "Publish" in the upper right-hand corner, and your room will be scheduled and available for other Clubhouse users to see.

This is another case where you can use the Notes app to include emojis appropriate to your description. If you're speaking in your zone of genius, it will be very helpful for you to understand the pain points, challenges, issues, concerns, questions, and goals that matter to your target audience. Use that information to create your headline and descriptive summary of your room.

You don't have to create everything from scratch even when you plan to be on the stage alone in your room. If you've given webinars, presentations, live talks, or seminars, you can repurpose that content for a Clubhouse room. Just keep in mind that, unlike most platforms, you won't have visuals to enhance your presentation.

You can also repeat the same presentation more than once as your following grows. At any given time, you'll have new followers who missed that presentation because they weren't following you yet, missed the notification, or simply couldn't make it. Give them another opportunity to hear it. I created a room titled "5 Strategies to Land a Job Quickly." It's a training I've given before, and I expect to give it several more times on Clubhouse.

People who follow you may be notified about your room, but don't depend on this to bring a significant audience to your room. Your followers might not have notifications turned on, or they might see the notification hours after you've already closed your room. A few people might stumble upon your room because of their interests and decide to join you, but hoping for random people to find your room isn't a plan. It's your job to promote the room.

An "if you build it, they will come" attitude on Clubhouse will only result in disappointment. A-list celebrities, like Drake and Ashton Kutcher, industry titans, like Mark Zuckerberg and Elon Musk, and social media influencers, whose communities have followed them to Clubhouse, won't have to promote their rooms much, but most of us don't have the luxury of spontaneously starting a room and having a significant audience show up. Be prepared to spread the word about your upcoming room.

Promote your room and its value on other social media platforms, where you may have a bigger audience of followers, friends, and connections. If you have an existing email list, announce the upcoming room to your subscribers. Tell people when the room will be open, who will be speaking, and what they can expect to get out of it. Remember to focus on what's in it for them. Give them a reason to show up. As the time for your room gets closer, share a reminder and invite people to come. You can also ping people on the Clubhouse app and invite them to join your room. And if other speakers are joining you onstage, suggest that they promote the room and invite people as well.

Do the work to get more people in the room, but don't despise small audiences. I once opened a room expecting dozens if not a few hundred people to show up, but my turnout was closer to thirty souls. I later found out people who had planned to attend hadn't been able to find the room. Whatever the reason for the low attendance, I gave those thirty people the same level of value I would've given a packed conference room. If you start a room and only two people show up, talk to them like you have an audience of two hundred or two thousand. They've taken time to show up for you, so make sure you show up for them.

Since this platform is audio-only, you'll never have to create a PowerPoint presentation, but you do need to plan your talks. First, decide what kind of presentation style you want to use. Popular set-ups include interview, panel talk, Q&A (question and answer) or AMA (ask me anything), and conversation (everyone talks). If you feel comfortable going it alone, you can do a solo presentation or a solo Q&A with the spotlight solely on you as the expert, but you'll also be *solely* responsible for holding the attention of the audience. Clubhouse is designed to inspire conversation and create connection, so don't get too caught up in being the sage on the stage.

Partnering with a friend or colleague for an interview, on the other hand, takes some of the responsibility off you and has the potential added benefit of bringing in the other person's followers, especially if your friend is willing to promote the room in advance. The same applies to panel talks. The different points of view, backgrounds, and personalities that come out when you have multiple people on stage can often better engage the audience and hold their attention for longer periods of time. Everyone likes to feel like they're in on a great conversation.

When it's time to start your room, show up like the leader you are. This is the space you've created. Be prepared, but don't overdo it. Clubhouse really should be fun, even if you're there with your career or business goals in mind. Discussing your area of expertise, sharing new ideas, and questioning the status quo—all this should be as enjoyable for you as it is productive.

If you invite other speakers or audience members to the stage, you may need to remind them to mute their mics so there's no background noise or cross talk. It's your job to make sure your room runs smoothly, so take responsibility for moderating your room or ask one of your speakers to be a moderator and then give them that power. Moderators have the same power you have, so don't just give it to anyone. You want someone to moderate who will remove trolls from the stage and mute and unmute people at appropriate times. It's best to ask people if they will help moderate your room in advance. And be skeptical of people you don't know who offer to moderate for you. An incompetent or scammy moderator can ruin your room.

START A CLUB

Starting your own club on Clubhouse is optional, but it can be a great way to increase your following and solidify your place as a leader and an expert. Similar to Facebook groups, a club on Clubhouse is a community within the larger community. Clubs are places for people with similar interests and goals to congregate for conversation.

I founded a club called "The Money Is on LinkedIn!" It's targeted at my ideal clients, professionals and entrepreneurs who want to earn more by advancing their career or growing their business. As I write this, the club has over 1,200 members (and 6,500 followers), and whenever I start a room in the club, all those people are notified and have an opportunity to join in.

Clubhouse clubs are a part of the larger social experiment being run by the app's algorithm. It's impossible to predict exactly how starting a club will impact your following, but it's a safe bet to say that impact will be positive. I've noticed that more people have followed me based on the information in my Club description, and I can only assume Clubhouse chose to show my club to them based on their interests.

As Clubhouse creators promised it would, starting a club has gotten easier, no longer requiring an application-approval process. To start a club, navigate to your profile and scroll down to the "Member of" section. There, you'll see a plus sign, which you can tap to start a club. (If you belong to several clubs, you may have to scroll through them to get to the plus sign.) You'll be asked for your club name and some details about your new club.

Clubhouse is still growing rapidly, and that includes the backend of the site, so this process, like any part of the app, is subject to change at any time. As of this writing, you can only create one club at a time, and just as important, you can't delete a club in-app. If you start the Dog Breeders Rock! club, and then decide to delete it because it has nothing to do with your career as a bank executive, you may have to jump through some hoops to get rid of it or you may be stuck with it.

When you start a club, if you choose to, you get to define the rules within the limits of Clubhouse's terms and conditions. Keep your rules simple and to the point. (I have three rules for my club.) Then, invite people who you believe will be interested in your club. Joining a club requires no more than the tap of an icon and isn't a big commitment, so people who know you or follow you are likely to join. The more conversations you have in your club, the more likely people are to find you and join. You can also define up to three topics for your club, which makes it easier to attract the right people.

Within your club, you have quite a bit of control. You can hide the members list from the public and even make it a private space by not allowing followers. This can be valuable if you and a group of colleagues, clients, or friends want a private place to share ideas and have conversations. Whatever kind of club you decide to start—if you choose to start one—you'll need to put time and effort into nurturing your membership. Craft a plan for the rooms you want to start, and add them to your schedule.

One important note. As the creator of a club, you can allow members to start their own rooms under the umbrella of your club. Proceed with caution on this one. Initially, you may know everyone in your club, but if it grows, it can quickly include members who are strangers to you. Any room started in your club can impact your reputation on and off the platform. For better or worse, those rooms are a reflection of you.

JOIN A CLUB

Following and joining other people's clubs can also benefit you by helping you grow your Clubhouse community. To follow a club, all you have to do is find the club and click "Follow." However, to join you must be nominated by a member or invited and then accept the club's rules. Members have some privileges followers don't have, such as nominating other users to become members of the club, and in some clubs, starting rooms.

Be clear on the rules for the club, and only start rooms within the club if you have permission from the club's creator or if they've made it clear that they welcome members to start rooms. Nominating members to a club is an opportunity to grow your community and contribute to the group by inviting people who would be a great fit for the club.

FINDING PLACES TO BE

When you're in the hallway, look at the bottom right-hand corner. There, you'll see a small group of dots with a larger green dot. Tap that icon, and if you've started or belong to any clubs, you'll see "Active Clubs" and a list of clubs that have rooms going on or active members in that moment. Below that you'll see "Available to Chat." When you and another user follow each other, you'll each appear in the others "Available to Chat" section.

If you see text below someone's name in "Available to Chat," that's the title of the room they're currently in. Tap on their name or profile pic, and you'll see an opportunity to start a closed room together or join the room they're listening to or speaking in. Starting a closed room will send an invitation to them, and they can choose to join you in the room or decline for the moment. Checking out where your contacts are currently spending time can be a great way to find rooms you want to join.

chapter 6
THE SECRET TO MAXIMIZING CLUBHOUSE

CEO of Strawberri Curls, Gabrielle Allen (@strawbericurls), was at a loss as to how to reach more of the people in her industry across the country, but Clubhouse provided the solution to her problem. Gabrielle found few experts from her industry on Clubhouse when she first joined, and she didn't hesitate to fill that vacuum. She started by joining rooms and adding value with her general business knowledge. Then, she focused in on her niche. "I started my own club called The Hair and Beauty Professional Club. And I started to focus more on hairstylists, the salon industry, and the beauty industry, versus just general business."

Gabrielle also leveraged SMS technology to grow her list of email subscribers, a valuable asset for any business. After establishing her credibility, she offered her opt-in gift (a free resource to help professionals build their salon or beauty industry business) from the stage. Rather than give them a link, which can be hard to remember, she shared a phone number and code word. Audience members texted the keyword to the given number, received the gift, and were added to Gabrielle's list. "I'm now sending more emails," says Gabrielle, "nurturing my list to eventually start doing virtual classes." Already a well-known natural hair stylist and salon owner, Clubhouse has allowed her to increase her visibility as a beauty profession educator.

VALIDATE AND LEVERAGE CLUBHOUSE WITH LINKEDIN

As Gabrielle grows her platform on Clubhouse, LinkedIn will be essential to her ability to assess potential partnerships, speaking opportunities, and even potential clients. I've already shared with you the best-kept secret to maximizing Clubhouse: strategic use of LinkedIn. Now, let's get into the how.

Adriane Simpson

Clubhouse is a bit like the Wild West of social media platforms right now. No one really knows how it will change in the coming months and years, nor do we know its full potential. By showing up consistently, you can stake out new territory that isn't owned by any particular expert yet. You can also show more of your authentic personality than other platforms allow within their limitations of print and video only.

The freedom Clubhouse provides all of us also allows people to portray themselves however they want, and that portrayal doesn't have to be based in truth. If someone on Clubhouse says they're a venture capitalist, the VP of Human Resources for a Fortune 500 company, or a seven-figure business owner, you have nothing but their word to go on. Don't be fooled into thinking a large following or sharing the stage with reputable people mean a particular person is who they say they are or that they've accomplished what they claim to have done.

That's where LinkedIn comes in. Now, don't get me wrong. It's certainly possible to create an exaggerated or completely fabricated resume on LinkedIn. It's even possible to connect with the right people and use their good reputation to bolster one's own. But it would take a lot of time and effort to pull that off. It's a lot easier for a scammer to shortcut to an audience on other platforms.

More than any other social media platform, LinkedIn is a reliable resource for verifying and validating what you see on Clubhouse.

Remember you're on Clubhouse to accomplish your professional and business goals. While you might set aside some of your free time to explore other interests on the app, that's secondary. You can't afford to waste time and energy on people who aren't adding real value. Before you start to build a relationship with someone you've connected with on Clubhouse, validate their claims with LinkedIn.

Start by searching for the person's name on LinkedIn. If he or she has a common name, and you don't have any contacts in common, you might have to do a little digging, but anyone serious about business should at least have a presence on the platform. Once you find the right person, click on their profile and examine the details. If this person purports to be a Senior VP of Marketing at Disney, then their LinkedIn profile should confirm that experience. The bottom line is that their LinkedIn presence should support and expand on who they say they are on Clubhouse, as should yours.

If you can't find the person on LinkedIn or their profile seems misaligned or out of date, then you can do deeper research by looking at their presence on other social media platforms, and of course, by searching for them on Google. In most cases, however, you should be able to get what you need from a simple LinkedIn search. At the same time, people who meet you on Clubhouse and who are serious about doing business with you will likely check you out on LinkedIn too. If you've followed the steps in Chapter 2, you'll be in good shape to make a positive professional impression.

LinkedIn is also essential for taking relationships beyond Clubhouse for another reason. As of this writing, Clubhouse doesn't have direct-message or comment functions. The only way to communicate with people is in a room, and when it's over, it's over. When you want to take the conversation further, you could open a private room and invite that person to talk, but that's a one-off chat and doesn't connect you two in an ongoing way even if they accept your invitation. It's much more effective to invite people to connect with you on LinkedIn. Yes, of course they can follow you on Instagram or Twitter, but these are often one-way follows and less of a relationship. LinkedIn connects you in a more reciprocal fashion.

When you connect with someone on LinkedIn, neither of you is following the other, so you're in a more equitable relationship. Even more important, connecting on LinkedIn signals that you're interested in some type of business relationship. You're not looking for dates. You're not looking for people to hang out with. You're looking to connect in a professional manner for the benefit of all involved.

Once someone you've met on Clubhouse either sends you an invitation to connect on LinkedIn or accepts your invitation, it's a good idea to follow-up with another personal message. Reference how you connected or the conversation you started on Clubhouse, and start a new conversation about how you can help each other achieve your goals. In this conversation, remember to give before you take. Depending on the person you're connecting with, you may offer to connect them with someone in your network or share your insights on a project they've mentioned. If you're a business owner, you can offer a sample of your product, a link to your free opt-in gift, a consultation call, or a virtual coffee chat to get to know each other better. Get creative and keep it professional.

When you're on stage in a room, and you've given value, you can expect to gain more followers on Clubhouse. You can also invite the people in the room to find you and connect on LinkedIn. They may be your potential customers or clients. They may be the people who can get you in the door for your dream job. And they've just seen you onstage with your expertise, your brilliance, and your passion for what you do on display. You're fresh in their minds, and if they want to know more about you, they're likely to connect with you on LinkedIn.

THE ELEPHANT IN THE ROOM

At the time of this writing, Clubhouse is just rolling out a beta test feature for some users of the app that will allow you to get paid by your listeners. Instead of peppering your Clubhouse bio with your CashApp, Venmo, or Zelle handles, your audience will have the option to pay you for expertise by clicking on your profile and then clicking on "Send Money." Adding your cash handles to your profile isn't a practice you see on LinkedIn, but it has become a cultural norm on Clubhouse. Even if you don't have any products to sell, you can still position yourself to be paid for your knowledge if you have the ability to receive payments and your listeners find your content valuable. We'll have to wait and see how this new feature plays out and if it becomes widely available.

I encourage you to always provide valuable content to any stage you grace, whether you're getting paid for your expertise or not. Remember: if you show up and add value, you will connect with your target audience. It doesn't matter if that audience is made up of recruiters looking for the next best candidate, customers in need of your services, or potential strategic partners.

Both Clubhouse and LinkedIn are ideal platforms for developing your personal and professional brands. In the same way that individuals and small business brands are taking advantage of these opportunities, larger organizations are also trying to figure out how to establish their presence on Clubhouse. Ironically, it can be more challenging for them since the app was created to feature individual voices over big company footprints.

One way Clubhouse creatives have leveraged this gap is by offering room sponsorship opportunities for companies that want to increase their number of followers and grow brand awareness. A company may hire an influencer to moderate a room that features discussions about the company's products and services, thereby speaking directly to an audience of potential new customers. In turn, listeners learn more about a new brand and begin the "know, like, and trust" process essential to all business success. If the sponsorship room is about a specific product, there should be associated sales the company can link directly to that discussion, further validating their return on any investment made. Companies are paying high dollar amounts to influencers, leveraging the same successful strategies I'm sharing with you in this book. Use them. They work!

THE FUTURE OF CLUBHOUSE AND LINKEDIN

I'm the first to say Clubhouse is a ground-breaking social media platform. There's no denying its meteoric growth or its impact on our culture. But at least for now, the site still has some limitations. Fortunately, those limitations are easily overcome when you pair your participation on Clubhouse with your presence on LinkedIn.

While I don't have a crystal ball or insider information, I foresee nothing but growth in Clubhouse's future, especially since the company has shown a willingness to evolve and expand. The company responded to privacy concerns by removing the requirement that users give the app access to their phone contacts and by giving early adopters the opportunity to have contacts deleted from the apps database. Clubhouse also has plans to make it easier to share links in your profile, which will appeal to those of us trying to monetize our Clubhouse presence. Finally, Clubhouse is showing its desire to support content creators with its Creator First program. Not surprisingly, the program is available only by invitation for now, but there's a good chance that this is just the beginning of the platform helping users find ways to monetize their presence there.

LinkedIn isn't going anywhere either. It remains a constant and stays in its lane as a professional networking site. At the same time, the developers of LinkedIn continue to innovate, making the platform easier to use. You might be tempted to skip LinkedIn and go straight to Clubhouse, the hottest new thing. That's certainly the easier course of action, but it will cost you. To make the most of Clubhouse, you need a place to validate people and businesses, connect one-on-one, and grow your relationships. Clubhouse provides a new audience and a new way to reach them. LinkedIn serves as a unique tool to leverage that audience for maximum value.

LinkedIn and Clubhouse have very different set-ups, and at first glance, it might appear that they're made for different audiences, but look a little deeper, and you'll find a perfect pairing. In fact, you can make more of both platforms when you use each to supplement the other. There's never been a better time or place to grow your business or expand your network. I'll see you on Clubhouse—and LinkedIn.

Visit bit.ly/ClubhouseQuickStart to download my free resource for readers. Use these downloads to start taking action, choose which strategies you'll use, and keep track of your progress.

RESOURCES

[1] Dean, Brian. "How Many Users Does Clubhouse Have? 40+ Clubhouse Stats (2021)." *Backlinko*, 22 Feb. 2021, backlinko.com/clubhouse-users.

[2] Osman, Maddy. "Mind-Blowing LinkedIn Statistics and Facts (2021)." *Kinsta*, 31 Dec. 2020, kinsta.com/blog/linkedin-statistics/.

[3] Osman, Maddy. "Mind-Blowing LinkedIn Statistics and Facts (2021)." *Kinsta*, March 9, 2021. https://kinsta.com/blog/linkedin-statistics/#:~:text=With%20more%20than%2020%20million,of%20recruiters%20regularly%20use%20LinkedIn.

[4] "Help." *Email Address Needed for an Invitation | LinkedIn Help*, www.linkedin.com/help/linkedin/answer/1239.